SPIDERS

BIRD-EATING SPIDERS

James E. Gerholdt
ABDO & Daughters

Published by Abdo & Daughters, 4940 Viking Drive, Suite 622, Edina, Minnesota 55435.

Library bound edition distributed by Rockbottom Books, Pentagon Tower, P.O. Box 36036, Minneapolis, Minnesota 55435.

Printed in the United States.

Cover Photo credit: Jim Gerholdt
Interior Photo credits: Jim Gerholdt

Edited by Julie Berg

Library of Congress Cataloging-in-Publication Data

Gerholdt, James E., 1943
   Bird-eating spider / by James E. Gerholdt.
      p.   cm. — (Spiders)
Includes bibliographical references (p.23) and index.
   ISBN 1-56239-507-6
1. Tarantulas—Juvenile literature. [1. Bird spiders. 2. Tarantulas. 3. Spiders.]   I. Title.
II. Series:
Gerholdt, James E., 1943- Spiders.
QL458.42.T5G46   1995
595.4'4—dc20   95-12366
                                                                       CIP
                                                                       AC

About the Author

Jim Gerholdt has been studying reptiles and amphibians for more than 40 years. He has presented lectures and displays throughout the state of Minnesota for 9 years. He is a founding member of the Minnesota Herpetological Society and is active in conservation issues involving reptiles and amphibians in India and Aruba, as well as Minnesota.

Contents

BIRD-EATING SPIDERS

Bird-eating spiders belong to one of the 84 spider **families**. Tarantulas are also included in this family.

A spider is an **arachnid**. It has two body parts and eight legs. All arachnids are **arthropods**. Their skeletons are on the outside of their bodies. Bird-eating spiders are also **ectothermic**. They get their body temperature from the **environment**.

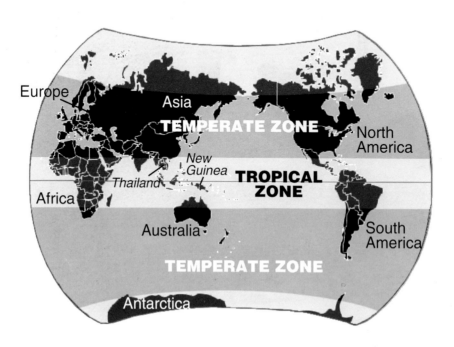

This salmon pink bird-eating spider comes from Brazil.

There are about 37,000 **species** of spiders in the world. About 800 of these are bird-eaters and tarantulas. They are found in the American **tropics**, Thailand, and New Guinea. They are large, hairy spiders with fangs that strike down.

The goliath bird-eating spider from South America is the world's largest spider.

SHAPES

Bird-eating spiders are very heavy bodied. Like tarantulas, they are also very hairy! They have two body parts that are almost round in shape. The head and **thorax** make up the front body part, called the **cephalothorax**.

The rear body part is called the **abdomen**. This is where the **spinnerets** are located. The spinnerets make the spider's silk. The eight legs and the **pedipalps** are

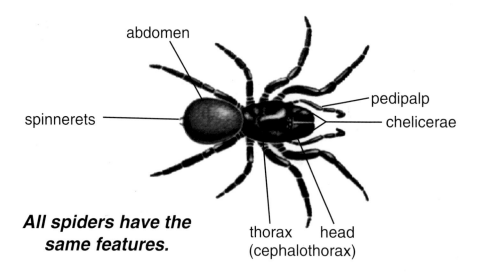

abdomen

spinnerets

pedipalp

chelicerae

thorax   head
(cephalothorax)

***All spiders have the
same features.***

You can see the eyes, and the pedipalps on this salmon pink bird-eating spider.

attached to the front of the body. The **pedipalps** look like two short legs. They are used to grab **prey**. Between the pedipalps are the **chelicerae**, to which the fangs are attached.

This Colombian bird-eating spider is brown.

This young goliath bird-eating spider is at home in the rainforest.

SENSES

Bird-eating spiders have the same five senses as humans. Like most spiders, they have eight eyes. But their eyesight is not very good. Since most **species** are active at night, their eyes are used to detect light levels.

The hairs of a bird-eating spider are very sensitive to **vibrations**. The hairs on their legs and **pedipalps** help them find the way through their **habitat**.

Bird-eating spiders can taste and smell the world around them with their mouth and the ends of the pedipalps and legs.

Notice the sensitive hairs on this young goliath bird-eating spider.

DEFENSE

Many of the bird-eating spiders use **camouflage** to defend themselves against their enemies. Even a brightly colored salmon pink bird-eating spider is hard to see in its **habitat**.

If the camouflage doesn't work, the spider may rear back and threaten the enemy. It will also bite! Even though the bite isn't fatal to a human, it hurts.

Bird-eaters also defend themselves by shedding their hairs. The hairs are very irritating to the skin of a human or **predator**. If the hairs get in the eyes, it is very painful.

This young Peruvian bird-eating spider blends into its habitat.

FOOD

Despite their name, bird-eating spiders usually don't eat birds. But when they do, the birds are babies, **nesting** or **roosting**. They also eat insects, other spiders, frogs, lizards, and snakes.

Bird-eaters are active hunters. They will eat any animal they can overpower. The spider grabs its **prey** with its **pedipalps** then bites with its fangs. The spider holds its prey until the poison takes effect. Once the prey has been killed, the spider sucks out all the fluids, leaving a shapeless mass!

A young Colombian bird-eating spider eating a cricket.

This young goliath bird-eating spider has just shed its skin.

GLOSSARY

Abdomen (AB-doe-men) - The rear body part of an arachnid.

Arachnid (uh-RACK-nid) - An arthropod with two body parts and eight legs.

Arthropod (ARTH-row-pod) - An animal with its skeleton on the outside of its body.

Bamboo - A grass plant with tall, hollow, woody stems.

Burrow (BUR-oh) - A hole or tunnel dug into the ground; also, to dig a burrow.

Camouflage (CAM-uh-flaj) - The ability to blend in with the surroundings.

Cephalothorax (seff-uh-low-THOR-ax) - The front body part of an arachnid.

Chelicerae (kel-ISS-err-eye) - The leg-like organs of a spider that have the fangs attached to them.

Ectothermic (ek-toe-THERM-ik) - Regulating body temperature from an outside source.

Environment (en-VI-ron-ment) - Surroundings in which an animal lives.

Family (FAM-i-lee) - A grouping of animals.

Habitat - The area in which an animal lives.

Humidity - The amount of water in the air.

Legspan - The distance between the tips of opposite legs on a spider.

Moulting (MOLE-ting) - The act of shedding the old skin.

Nesting - An animal living in a nest.

Pedipalps (PED-uh-palps) - The two long sense organs on the head of an arachnid.

Predator (PRED-a-tore) - An animal that eats other animals.
Prey - An animal killed or hunted by another animal for food.
Rainforest - A dense, tropical forest that gets lots of rain.
Roosting - A bird at rest.
Species (SPEE-seas) - A kind or type.
Spinnerets (spin-err-ETS) - The two body parts attached to the abdomen of a spider where the silk is made.
Thorax (THORE-axe) - Part of the front body part of an arachnid.
Tropics - A region of the Earth that is very warm and often rainy.
Vibration (vie-BRAY-shun) - A trembling or quivering motion.

BIBLIOGRAPHY

de Vosjoli, Philippe. *Arachnomania - The General Care and Maintenance of Tarantulas and Scorpions.* Advanced Vivarium Systems, 1991.

Levi, Herbert W. and Lorna R. *Spiders and Their Kin.* Golden Press, 1990.

O'Toole, Christopher (editor). *The Encyclopedia of Insects.* Facts On File, Inc., 1986.

Preston-Mafham, Rod and Ken. *Spiders of the World.* Facts On File, Inc., 1984.

Webb, Ann. *The Proper Care of Tarantulas.* T.F.H. Publications, Inc., 1992.

Index